Guildhall of Corpus Christi Lavenham

Suffolk

THE NATIONAL TRUST

Above The oriel window on the Lady Street façade

Right The porch

LAVENHAM GUILDHALL

LAVENHAM GUILDHALL, properly known as the Guildhall of Corpus Christi, is one of the finest timber-framed buildings in Britain, and reflects the great wealth of Lavenham's early 16th-century heyday. A document of 1596 describes it as 'fair' in appearance, and it would have impressed Tudor visitors much as it impresses us today.

The majority of Lavenham's timber buildings, and almost all the larger merchants' houses, date from between about 1460 and about 1530. On stylistic grounds, the Corpus Christi Guildhall probably dates from around 1530. It was among the last to be constructed before the crash which turned the boom town of the early 16th century into an economic backwater within a single generation. After about 1530 the townsmen built only a few smaller tenements and demolished many of the greater houses which they could no longer afford to maintain. By the beginning of the 17th century the situation was so severe that Lavenham's lord of the manor took his tenants to court, complaining that not a single house would be left standing, if the destruction continued. The best merchants' houses, built with similar or even greater emphasis on display than the Guildhall, were lost at that time.

Since 1951 the Guildhall has been in the care of the National Trust, together with two adjacent properties, 26 and 27 Market Place, which currently house a gift shop, library and tea-room. Together, these three buildings represent a remarkably well-preserved section of late medieval street, and offer important insights into the economic, domestic and religious life of the early Tudor period.

Above The mummified remains of a cat were discovered in a nearby roof. It would have been placed there to protect the building's owner from evil spirits

Left The plainer rear façade of the Guildhall was largely reconstructed in the early 20th century. Today, it looks down on a tranquil courtyard garden

LAVENHAM AND THE CLOTH INDUSTRY

Below The Guildhall occupies the southern (upper) side of Lavenham's Market Place

Below right The Luttrell Psalter shows women spinning and carding wool

Opposite The wealthy cloth merchant Thomas Spring II

The timber-framed streets for which Lavenham is justly famous cannot be understood without reference to the industry which made the town great, and eventually consigned it to relative poverty.

Already by 1327, Lavenham was an industrial town specialising in the production of woollen cloth. Its regular street pattern reveals an element of urban planning, probably by the powerful De Vere family, Earls of Oxford, who possessed the manor and stimulated its commercial activity. The weaving and finishing of woollen cloth had been a speciality of the region since at least the 12th century. Other nearby towns such as Sudbury, Hadleigh and Long Melford shared in the industry, but were less dependent upon it than Lavenham. Although sheep were farmed locally, they were not present in large numbers. Contrary to popular myth, the surrounding countryside was primarily arable, as it is today, and most of the raw wool was bought in from places such as Lincolnshire, where the soil was better suited to sheep farming. Home-grown wool was of relatively poor quality, and was used for such purposes as stuffing mattresses. Lavenham was not a *wool town*, but a *woollen town*.

The 15th century saw Lavenham share disproportionately in the growth of the export market in woollen cloth. Only the most successful entrepreneurs were able to exploit these overseas markets, and the profits of the industry became concentrated in the hands of fewer and fewer individuals. These successful merchants, who could each employ more than a hundred spinners, weavers and other craftsmen, were known as clothmakers or clothiers. They congregated together in the larger towns, where they could share expensive resources such as dyehouses, while their employees often lived in the smaller villages nearby. By 1524 Lavenham was the fourteenth wealthiest town in England, paying more tax in that year than much more populous cities such as Lincoln and York. It paid three times more than its nearest rivals Sudbury and Long Melford, and specialised in the production of woad-dyed broadcloth known as Lavenham Blues.

Lavenham's enormous wealth, derived almost exclusively from woollen cloth, enabled its merchants to rebuild their houses and church in flamboyant style. Only the smaller properties, usually owned by cloth merchants, but rented out to poorer tenants, escaped this great rebuilding. Yet such was the dependence of the town upon a single industry that it was especially vulnerable to the recession which hit cloth manufacturing in the 1520s and 1530s. European wars interrupted key export markets and, coupled with the heavy taxation which followed, forced the clothiers to lay off their workforce. As early as 1525 Lavenham saw demonstrations by unemployed men and women several thousand strong. The bubble of success had burst, and many merchant families left the industry to invest in land and join the gentry, taking their vital capital with them. By 1568 Lavenham ranked well behind other local towns such as Sudbury and Nayland, and had only its buildings to remind it of former glories.

MILLIONAIRE MERCHANTS
Lavenham's pre-eminence is amply demonstrated by the number of merchants living there who would today be regarded as millionaires. In the early 16th century a skilled artisan earned four or fivepence per day, and was rarely able to save more than a few shillings. A merchant with £10 in disposable assets would be regarded as wealthy, and anyone with more than £50 was rich indeed. In 1522, shortly before the construction of the Guildhall, Lavenham boasted 24 such individuals, of whom no fewer than 21 were clothiers. A total of 33 cloth merchants lived in the town, all but one worth more than £10. The wealthiest of all the Lavenham merchants, Thomas Spring III, was valued at a phenomenal £3,200.

Above On feast days, gild members would have processed through the passageway beneath the west tower of East Bergholt church, Suffolk

Right The Wenhaston Doom. St Michael weighs the souls of the dead, while the Devil looks on, in the early 16th-century painting of the Last Judgement in Wenhaston church, Suffolk

MEDIEVAL GILDS

Despite the importance of the cloth industry in the town, Lavenham's five recorded gilds were not concerned with the organisation of trade. Craft gilds did exist in medieval England, but were generally confined to the larger towns and cities. The great majority were social and religious bodies, which dealt more with their members' souls than their livelihoods. (This guide uses the original spelling of the word gild.)

Well over 500 gilds are known to have existed in medieval Suffolk, with even small villages often possessing several. The earliest recorded examples date from the late Anglo-Saxon period, and numbers seem to have steadily increased until 1547, when they were forcibly abolished during the Reformation. The soul, as conceived by the medieval church, was destined to suffer torment in Purgatory in order to atone for sins committed on earth before it could pass into Heaven. Performing good works on earth would shorten this period, as would intercession by the living on behalf of the dead. Prayers for the dead were therefore important for the repose of the soul, but, when performed by members of the priesthood, came at a price. Wealthy individuals could afford to establish private chantries in their parish churches for the purpose. Thomas Spring III of Lavenham left money in his will for a thousand masses to be 'songen for the welth of my soule' immediately after his death. For the majority, however, such chantries or private masses were too expensive, and they subscribed instead to local gilds, whose collective funds could then be used to hire priests to recite the names of all members.

Gilds also served to regulate the devotional lives of their members and provide a secular link between the individual and the church. Each gild organised celebrations on the annual feast day of its patron saint, perhaps in the form of plays illustrating the saint's life or processions around the church and town. Much of the year might be spent rehearsing these performances and preparing costumes for them. The image of the saint in the parish church, whether in the form of a statue or painting, would be maintained during the year and lit by candles. Gilds would also raise money to repair the church fabric, often by organising a Church Ale at which members brewed and sold ale, often performing a play at the same time.

Having paid their joining fees and regular subscriptions, members could expect to borrow money from the collective purse, or be provided with a pension, if they fell on hard times. Entry fees varied enormously, ranging from an insignificant threepence to an expensive fourteen shillings, and it is likely that an element of social prestige was attached to the membership of particular gilds.

SERVING MANY NEEDS

In the modern world, the functions of medieval gilds are provided by many different bodies, ranging from the local private golf club to amateur dramatics societies and fund-raising committees, insurance companies and the Welfare State.

Below Thomas Spring III, the wealthiest cloth merchant in Lavenham, paid for this magnificent private chapel, or parclose, in the church

GILDHALLS

Some gilds met in private houses, or in part of the parish church, but as incomes increased during the later Middle Ages, many were able to afford purpose-built gildhalls. These might be exclusive to a particular gild, or shared by several. Surviving halls of this kind are not uncommon in East Anglia, and typically contain at least one large meeting room where all gild members could assemble at least once a year to hold their 'Annual General Meeting' and banquet. The officers of the society would be selected at these meetings. On other occasions, the hall might be used to rehearse plays, or leased for events such as wedding feasts in much the same way as a village hall is used today.

Gildhalls are usually located close to parish churches, enabling gild members to process easily between the two and make use of the churchyard for their performances. Lavenham's four gildhalls are notable exceptions to this, perhaps indicating the importance of the Market Place in the life of the town. As they generally occupy valuable commercial sites, the meeting halls of most surviving examples are on the first floor, enabling the ground floors to be let as shops or domestic accommodation. Gildhalls are almost always unheated, though some may have separate kitchens and brew-houses. The gildhall at Bassingbourne in Cambridgeshire contained enough plates and dishes in 1546 to feed over a hundred people, and many, even in small villages, are large enough to have accommodated many more. The gild of the rural parish of Bardwell in Suffolk had well over a hundred members in the early 16th century and included a minstrel and cook among its officers. Gildhalls reflected both the status of the gild and that of the parish as a whole, and are usually very ornate both internally and externally. Fine roofs, rivalled only by ecclesiastical buildings, are found in many, and neighbouring parishes evidently copied and attempted to outshine each other's halls. Fine examples may be seen close to their respective churches at nearby Hadleigh and Stoke-by-Nayland.

At the Reformation gilds were abolished, and their property, which could be considerable, confiscated by the Crown. Gilds were directly associated with the maintenance of images and ideas which the Protestant faith saw as superstitious and idolatrous.

Right Gildhalls were potent status symbols and so were often elaborately decorated inside and out

FORGOTTEN BUT NOT GONE
After the Reformation, many gildhalls were either demolished, converted for domestic or commercial purposes, or repurchased from the Crown to serve as town halls or other public buildings. A number were dismantled and re-erected on farms, where they served as barns. Many remain undiscovered, long since disguised as houses or rows of cottages, and betrayed only by spectacular roof timbers concealed within.

Left Hadleigh gildhall

Right Lavenham's massive church of St Peter and St Paul is a vivid reminder of the town's prosperity in the late 15th century

LAVENHAM'S GILDS AND GILDHALLS

Five gilds are mentioned in the wills of Lavenham residents between 1416 and 1540, dedicated to the Holy Trinity, Saints Peter and Paul, the Assumption of Our Lady, St Christopher and Corpus Christi. Relatively few wills survive before the middle of the 15th century, and more gilds may have existed at different times. This number of gilds is by no means unusual in a town of this size, but it is surprising, and a reflection of Lavenham's wealth, that at least four of them possessed separate halls.

The earliest mention of a gild in Lavenham appears in the 1416 will of John Carpenter, who bequeathed 40 shillings to the Holy Trinity gild. Thereafter references are found with increasing regularity until the last in 1540. The Trinity gild was left money in 1469 to endow a chaplain to celebrate mass in the church on behalf of its brothers and sisters, and the same bequest included six almshouses in Church Street. The tenancies of these almshouses were placed at the disposal of the gild's alderman, and were said in a survey of 1596 to have been used 'in time past for the relief of the poore of the brotherhood of the Holye Trynitie'. The almshouses became parish property after the Reformation. The gild possessed two additional cottages in the High Street, and a gildhall which stood at the top of Prentice Street on what is now vacant ground behind the Angel Hotel. A bequest of 1494 concerns a cooking pot, presumably for the gildhall kitchen. The building, reputedly demolished as recently as 1879, was granted in 1533/4 through the manorial court to a number of trustees who held it on behalf of the gild. Since the hall is mentioned long before this date, the grant probably concerned only the legal status of the existing building rather than any new construction. A similar grant of 1529/30 relates to the Guildhall of Corpus Christi, and has often been used to date its structure. While the Guildhall does indeed appear to have been built around this time, we should treat the manorial grant with caution in the light of the Trinity reference. The Earls of Oxford retained manorial rights in the Trinity gildhall after the Reformation, accepting Thomas Larke, gentleman, as tenant in 1552 and Robert Rookewood Esquire in 1585.

The gild of Saints Peter and Paul possessed its own priest as early as 1446, and seems to have been the most popular of the town's gilds. Its hall, which was repaired in 1526, stood at the top of the High Street, a little above no. 21, and was demolished in 1896. Lavenham church bears the same dedication, suggesting a close link between gild and parish. John Risby left 6s 8d to it in 1493 on condition its brethren allowed him to join on his deathbed, and this sum may represent the normal entry fee. This gild owned cooking equipment, and in 1488 even a stall in the market place, which it presumably rented out.

Above The hall of the gild of Our Lady is believed to stand, albeit much altered, on the corner of Lady Street and Water Street. It was used as a wool hall in the early 18th century, when the town specialised in producing yarn.

Left The former gildhall of St Peter and St Paul prior to its demolition in 1896

THE GILD OF CORPUS CHRISTI

THE 1596 SURVEY OF LAVENHAM

First

one mesuage or faier tenement in the Market place of lavenh[a]m late in the tenure of Alan Sturmyn w[hi]ch mesuage in the one & twentie yeare of the reigne of Kinge Henry the eight late Kinge of Englande [1529–30] the lord did graunte* to myles Wytton and others of the Brotherhoode of the gylde of Corpus Christi, lienge next Barbors strete, or Reymestrete, or Griges strete, or Maister Johns strete on the west part rentinge yearlie xijd [12d]

Allso

one mesuage late in the tenure of Alan Sturmyn, the north heade abbuttinge on the Market place of lavenham & renteth vijd [7d]

* A legal nicety. The Earl of Oxford did not in fact present the site to the gild

Right The 1596 survey of Lavenham, which helps us to date the building of the Guildhall to 1529/30

The most remarkable aspect of the extensive documentary information concerning Lavenham's gilds is the lack of material relating to the Corpus Christi gild. Only two bequests have been traced in the surviving wills. Robert Parson left 6s 8d to it in 1477, and in 1520 Miles Wytton, a clothier, left a house in the High Street to his wife Margaret with instructions that it should pass on her death to the gild of Corpus Christi and the church of Lavenham. The Corpus Christi gild was evidently in being by 1477, at which date the present hall could not have existed. Did it possess an earlier hall on the same site or elsewhere, or did it meet in the church, as the link between the two institutions in Wytton's bequest might suggest? More intriguing still is the question of why a gild which clearly possessed great wealth should have attracted so few bequests.

The 'faier tenement' or beautiful house mentioned in the first entry from the 1596 survey of Lavenham is clearly the Guildhall (the various alternative names for the modern Lady Street deriving from its earlier chief residents), and the second entry is presumably 26 or 27 Market Place or both. The two properties had been held from the lord of the manor by Alan Sturmyn before one of them was given in 1529–30 to the Corpus Christi gild. This seems to give us a convincing date for the construction of the Guildhall, which fits perfectly with the stylistic evidence. Alan Sturmyn is described as a mercer in 1522, worth an impressive £80 (the thirteenth wealthiest merchant in the town), and inherited three properties from his father William in 1493. Perhaps two of them, or even all three, formed the southern block of the Market Place, which is the subject of this guide. Sturmyn would have been at least 57 years old in 1530. We have no record of his death, but may speculate that he donated his property in the Market Place to the Corpus Christi gild, perhaps with sufficient funds to build the new hall.

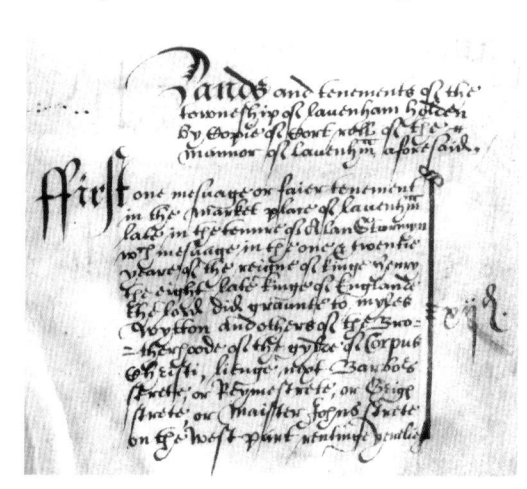

Evidence within the Guildhall also confirms that it was purpose-built for the gild, and is not, for example, a conversion of Sturmyn's house. The key point here is the lack of any heating in the hall, a feature firmly associated with public buildings and never found in domestic examples. The remarkable size of the original meeting hall, at just twelve feet in length smaller than those of most ordinary houses in Lavenham, may also explain the lack of bequests. The hall affords no room for the numbers expected at the meetings of most gilds, and membership must have been very low. Was Lavenham's Corpus Christi gild the most exclusive gild of all, taking members only from the town's merchant elite? Such an interpretation would also explain the enormous size of the Guildhall, and in particular its large attic space, which may have served as a warehouse.

CELEBRATING CORPUS CHRISTI
The festival of Corpus Christi, or the body of Christ, became ever more popular as the 15th century progressed, and many new gilds were founded to celebrate it. Its festival day, on the Thursday of the second week after Whit Sunday, usually fell in early June and can be compared with a modern village fête or carnival. The body of Christ in the form of the consecrated host was paraded through the streets for all to see amidst scenes of great jollity, with play cycles and other entertainments to follow. In many cities it became the major civic event of the year, akin to a Lord Mayor's Show. Given the importance of the event, it is doubly remarkable that the Gild of Corpus Christi failed to attract more notice in the wills of townsmen.

Left A Corpus Christi feast day procession from the Lovel Lectionary (British Library)

Above Sir William Cuthbert Quilter

A WARTIME WELCOME
During the Second World War the building welcomed visitors from all over Britain and beyond. Young evacuees from blitzed London were brought here before going on to temporary homes close by. The British Red Cross ran a restaurant providing meals and snacks for service men and women stationed locally.

THE GUILDHALL AFTER THE REFORMATION

Of Lavenham's four gildhalls only that of the Corpus Christi gild became parish property after the Reformation. The process by which this occurred is uncertain. The building may have been purchased from the Crown, as occurred elsewhere, but this may not have been necessary. The hall of a society of wealthy and influential merchants, perhaps concerned as much with civic government as religious matters, may not have been confiscated. The Corpus Christi gild's unusual status would certainly have made it easier to argue that its hall should become town property rather than swell the coffers of the State.

By 1689 the Guildhall, or part of it, was in use as a jail. In 1784 the prison reformer John Howard described its disrepair, two inmates having recently escaped by breaking through the plaster walls. This possibility, inevitable in a timber-framed structure, had obliged the local magistrates to secure their prisoners with thumb-screws. Closed as a jail in 1787, the hall was subsequently used as a workhouse, almshouse and warehouse before its purchase in 1887 by Sir William Cuthbert Quilter, Baronet, at one time MP for Sudbury. Quilter restored the building and was responsible for new additions to the rear. During the Second World War it received evacuees and served at varying times as a British Restaurant and nursery school. In 1946 Quilter's son, Sir William Eley Cuthbert Quilter, vested it in five local trustees to be held for the benefit of the people of Lavenham and the surrounding district. The property was vested in the National Trust in 1951. The Guildhall, which now houses a museum of local history and is used for various social functions, is today managed by a committee of local people whose members are nominated by the Trust and elected locally.

Left Preparing food in the Guildhall. The building was, and still is, a social centre for the town

Below The Guildhall in the 19th century, before Sir William Cuthbert Quilter's restoration

TIMBER-FRAMED CONSTRUCTION

The Guildhall and its associated buildings are fine examples of the medieval and Tudor tradition of timber-framing. East Anglia, in common with many other parts of Britain, lacks naturally occurring stone, and timber was the obvious choice of building material for all but the highest status structures. The timber was used green and unseasoned, typically felled only a few months before building work commenced. Each component of the frame was made on site or in a carpenter's yard, and the actual process of erecting or raising the frame would then take no more than a few days. It is a sobering thought, five centuries later, that while the Guildhall might have taken its carpenters many months to prefabricate, it would have been built within a week.

Despite its wealth of timber buildings, East Anglia was not heavily wooded. Only some 15% of the Suffolk landscape was woodland in 1086, and by 1349 this had fallen to 5%, though the proportion subsequently increased, as agricultural land was abandoned after the Black Death. In order to satisfy the great demand for timber and firewood, the limited woodland was intensively managed by a process known as coppicing. The majority of trees in a given area were cut down every few years, yielding crops of poles and brushwood from their sprouting stumps, while a number were permitted to grow through several felling cycles to produce larger timber. Coppiced trees grew much faster and straighter than hedgerow examples, benefiting from well-established root systems and obliged by a surrounding thicket of poles to grow upwards towards the light. The majority of timber found in East Anglian buildings grew for no more than 20 or 30 years, and even the largest posts and joists rarely contain over 70 or 80 annual growth rings.

When the frame of a structure had been raised, its walls were sealed with panels of wattle and daub, consisting of coppice poles and laths sprung between the timbers and thickly plastered with a mixture of clay and straw. A thin coat of lime plaster was then applied to the inner and outer surfaces of these panels, and the walls were complete. No external paint or plaster was applied, and, once the Guildhall had stood for a few months and the weather had turned its oak timbers from brown to grey, it would have appeared much as it does at present. Limewash was often applied as a sealant and preservative in more recent centuries. The painting or tarring of the timber frame to create a pattern of black and white is not a local tradition, and was introduced only in the Victorian period. The Guildhall's roof, like most in Lavenham, was tiled from the outset. Thatch was reserved in this area for agricultural buildings and houses of lower status, though wooden shingles were not uncommon.

Each individual timber of the frame was attached to its neighbours by joints of varying types, of which the simple mortise and tenon was the most common. Most of these joints were additionally secured with wooden spikes or pegs, the presence of which can often reveal the positions of original timbers, even where they have been removed or concealed. Features such as doors and windows can often be readily identified, despite subsequent alterations, and timber-framed buildings are ideal subjects for architectural and historical analysis.

Above The spaces between the timber-framing are filled with wattle and daub – interwoven laths covered in a mixture of clay and straw

Right A carved frieze in the Old Grammar School reveals the quality of late medieval woodwork in Lavenham

Opposite The roof timbers of the Guildhall

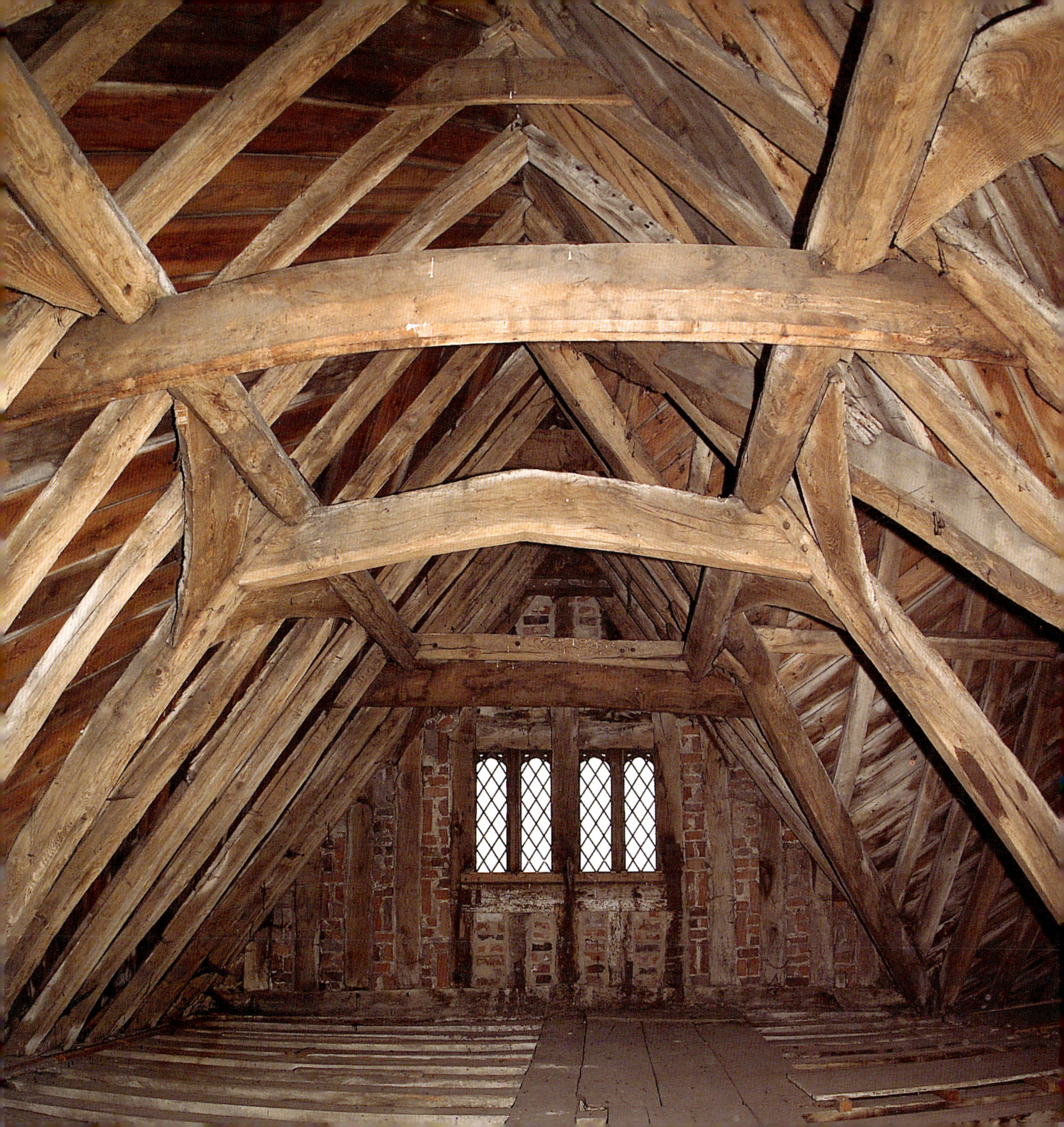

CONSPICUOUS CARVING

The Guildhall's exuberant carving is the principal feature which sets it apart from its nearest rivals. The carved post at the corner of Lady Street and the Market Place is often said to depict the 15th Earl of Oxford, the lord of the manor when the Guildhall was built, but this is unlikely. Posts of this type are known as *dragon* posts (a corruption of *diagonal*), as they support the dragon beams of the ceiling within. They are often beautifully carved with mythical or Biblical figures, such as Hercules, reflecting their conspicuous positions. The staff in the figure's right hand is very similar to that held by the *wodewose*, or man of the woods, who supports the hall ceiling of the Bull Hotel in nearby Long Melford, and an interpretation such as this is much the more likely.

THE EXTERIOR

The property in the care of the National Trust occupies the entire southern side of the Market Place and consists of three early 16th-century buildings which initially had no connection with each other. Their distinct roof lines are best viewed from a distance. The lowest roof, to the left (no. 26), is now a tea-room, but was originally a typical domestic house with a shop at one end. The structure in the centre of the row with the highest roof (no. 27) is another domestic house, of which the left-hand half is occupied by the town library and the right-hand by the present Guildhall entrance and gift shop. The hall of the Corpus Christi gild lies to the right of no. 27 beneath a slightly lower roof and includes the gable on the corner of Lady Street. The house to the rear of the Guildhall with separate access from Lady Street was also part of the building. The three component parts of this remarkable Tudor street may also be distinguished by their slightly different alignments, following the curved boundary of the Market Place.

All three buildings are jettied and close-studded, demonstrating the concern of the period with external as well as internal display. The use of so much expensive timber, with panels of wattle and daub just a few inches wide between the wall studs, was not structurally necessary. Early medieval buildings and even contemporary rural examples used much less, often plastering the frame externally. The practise of jettying, where upper storeys jut out and overhang lower storeys, also owes more to its dramatic visual impact than to any spacial or structural advantage; buildings are rarely jettied to the rear where they cannot be appreciated by passers-by.

The porch is a *tour de force*, one of the finest timber structures to survive from the period, and is the original main entrance. To the right of the porch, between it and the hall window, was the original access from the Market Place into the cellar beneath a low-arched opening in the front wall. It has since been blocked and disguised.

The modern entrance door into the Guildhall has been cut through the wall of the adjacent structure (no. 27). Close analysis of the stud pegs and other subtle features reveals an original oriel window in the position now occupied by the entrance and window of the town library, and a door to its right. The jetty timbers of this, and the building used as a tea-room, are carved in a similar but less elaborate style than those of the Guildhall.

The third and final structure of the complex (no. 26) was once jettied along its full length, but the right-hand half has since been underbuilt. Although the studding here is a little lighter and more widely spaced than elsewhere in the row, this can be explained rather by the slightly lower status of the house than by any significant difference in date. The building contained three rooms on its ground floor and reflects the classic cross-passage arrangement discussed on p.20. The right-hand of the two adjacent doors is the main entrance into the Tudor house, while the narrow door to its left served a shop with two arch-headed windows, through which goods were sold, much like a market stall.

Of the various types of late medieval shop fronts, this, containing two windows and a narrow door, was by far the most common. As shopkeepers were naturally keen to maximise their selling and display space, the width of their shop doors was kept to a minimum. The external hinged shutters here, the lower leaves forming counters by day, are probably no earlier than the 19th century.

Top The varying rooflines reflect the fact that the south side of the Market Place was originally three buildings

Above No.26 Market Place, the furthest left of the three houses that form the south side of the Market Place

THE INTERIOR

THE SERVICE ROOM
(*present Reception Room*)
This contains a fine roll-moulded ceiling and a large brick fireplace against its rear wall. This room was originally reached only from the hall, by means of the arched doorway which still survives. The fireplace dates from the 17th century, although it occupies the position of an original chimney, which may also have served a small kitchen to the rear. Notice the marks on the timber lintel, where rushlights or candles used to illuminate the cooking process have fallen or burnt down too far and scorched its surface.

This room occupies the position of the service area in the normal domestic plan, and would typically be divided into two rooms, as found in both the adjacent houses. Undivided service rooms were not uncommon, however. Rooms of this type were probably places of business, in this case probably a committee room for gild purposes.

Right The Hall and Parlour are now one room

The Hall

The service room and hall are linked by a fine doorway with a carved four-centred arch. On stepping through it, one is immediately impressed by the large and imposing space of the modern hall. However, this has been achieved only by removing an original partition which divided it into two much smaller rooms.

The original entrance to the Guildhall was through the porch. As in domestic houses of the period, the Tudor visitor would have stepped from the porch into a cross-passage between the front and rear doors of the hall. This cross-passage was partly divided from the hall by a pair of boarded screens, for which only the mortises remain in the door jambs. Close examination of the ceiling and wall timbers between the two windows which open onto the Market Place reveals evidence of the original partition between the hall and a separate parlour, which occupied the corner of the building. If we mentally reinstate the partition between hall and parlour, the true proportions of the Corpus Christi gild's hall become clear. A respectable 5.2m wide, it was no more than 4.3m long against the Market Place (discounting the cross-passage). Can we still accept that this was the meeting and banqueting hall of a wealthy institution? The absence of a fireplace from the hall – a feature associated only with public buildings – confirms that it was. Hearths were associated with domestic life and were not expected in public meeting halls, any more than in churches. The ground-floor windows of the Guildhall were almost certainly glazed, unlike those of most domestic houses at this period, so the lack of heating is unlikely to have caused any great hardship. The tables would have been arranged much like those of a traditional college dining hall, with the chief officers of the gild seated on a dais against the lost partition wall to the parlour and facing the cross-entry. Other members would be seated in the body of the hall.

Although the hall ceiling is beautifully moulded, it is plain compared with the exuberance of the exterior carving. Perhaps the calculating business minds of the gild members can be detected here: their building is certainly more concerned with external appearances.

The Parlour

In domestic situations the room beyond the high end of the hall was the principal bedroom of the house. Whether this room was used as a more private meeting area or perhaps even a bedroom for a gild official is impossible to determine.

The chimney at the rear of the Guildhall parlour is a later insertion, which also heats 1 Lady Street and interrupts both ceiling joists and wall studs. The evidence of a truncated trimmer joist suggests that a smaller chimney formerly existed here, containing a single fireplace to heat only the parlour. The surviving chimney retains its original red ochre pigment, common to all early brickwork, with its individual bricks picked out in white to disguise the irregular colouring of early bricks. This room contained the largest space on the ground floor, albeit rather narrow in its irregular proportions. Note the diagonal *dragon beam* in the ceiling, carrying the jetty joists to both Lady Street and Market Place, and the moulded mullions of the only oriel window to survive unrestored.

MEETING PLACE OR WAREHOUSE?

The great puzzle of Lavenham Guildhall concerns the provision of so much storage space in a building with a relatively small hall. If a dozen or so members of the Corpus Christi gild held occasional meetings and feasts in the hall, what happened in the five extensive rooms on the first floor, not to mention the cellar and the exceptionally large attic?

Unlike most gildhalls, the arrangement of the upper rooms here is very similar to those of contemporary merchants' houses which were used mainly for storage. The Guildhall's wide stair, which afforded access to the first floor without troubling the occupants of the hall, strongly suggests that its capacious upper rooms served as warehousing.

Was the Guildhall then as much a giant, ostentatious warehouse, as a meeting place for gild members? One of the chief pleasures of this magnificent structure is that we may never know for sure.

The Cellar

A door in the back wall of the hall leads down to a substantial brick cellar. Notice the underside of the stair to the first floor, now painted white; the treads of this stair are original, consisting of solid triangular blocks of oak which have been covered with modern boards.

Where they have escaped rebuilding, the walls of the cellar, which extends under both hall and parlour, are lined with arched niches and cupboards, which were intended to hold lamps, bottles and anything else which needed to be kept clear of the potentially damp floor. The cellar could also once be reached directly from the Market Place via a trap-door in the ceiling. As in a modern pub, the casks of wine and ale to be consumed by the gild members were presumably rolled down a ramp from the Market Place and, suitably decanted, made their final journey up the back stair.

The First Floor

The five rooms on the Guildhall's upper storey could be reached by the existing stair, either from the hall or directly from the rear courtyard without entering the ground-floor rooms. The exceptional width of the stair indicates that bulky objects were required to negotiate it, and the relatively spartan decoration upstairs suggests that this area was used for storage.

The landing at the top of the stair gave access to three separate rooms, and probably to the large attic space as well. A pair of arched doorways, which still survive, lead into the two rooms above the hall and parlour (Rooms 1 and 2 on the plan), and a third door reached the chamber above no. 1 Lady Street, which was also part of the Guildhall. A further two rooms lay above the service room and kitchen, making a grand total of five on the first floor.

The rebates above the windows would have housed sliding internal shutters in the absence of glass. The wooden lintel of the fireplace in Room 1 is incised with a pattern resembling a six-petalled flower in a circle. Identical marks, often known as daisy-wheels, are found on many fireplaces and associated with 17th-century ritual magic and the protection of vulnerable chimneys, which could not be physically closed at night against evil spirits. The small chamber over the porch was used in domestic houses to store valuables, and the finely moulded ceiling of the Guildhall's example suggests it was no exception. The fine linenfold panelling now displayed in the porch chamber is roughly contemporary with the building and is reputed to have once lined the walls of the parlour below.

The model in Room 1 is a scale reconstruction of the Guildhall as first built.

Above The fireplace lintel in Room 1 is carved with a daisy-wheel motif – a ritual symbol designed to ward off evil spirits

Left The Cellar

Opposite The alcove over the porch on the first floor is lined with early linenfold panelling

27 Market Place
(*Rooms 5 and 6: Gift Shop and Library*)
Rooms 5 and 6 of the Guildhall's upper storey are not part of the Guildhall proper, but belong to a neighbouring domestic house of similar date. Room 6 contains fragments of an early 17th-century plaster ceiling decorated with hearts or petals and shapes resembling *fleurs de lis*.

The ground floor contains a hall, with evidence of a cross-passage and a large oriel window in its front wall (the Library) and a pair of service rooms which now contain the shop. Notice the empty mortises in the shop's ceiling, which contained the removed partition between the two service rooms. The rear part of the hall (now the gentlemen's lavatory) is partitioned from the front and, unusually, appears to have accommodated a chimney stack within the exceptional width of the roof (7.6m). Early chimney stacks were often timber-framed, and this device would have protected any such feature from the weather. The house occupies a narrow building plot, and does not appear to have possessed a parlour (although the space around the chimney may have been used for this purpose).

26 Market Place (*Tea-room*)
This building offers the best opportunity within the Guildhall complex to understand a standard domestic house of the early Tudor period. Considerable numbers of very similar buildings survive in Lavenham and other market towns in the region.

The house follows the usual tripartite domestic plan, with a parlour, central hall, cross-passage and twin service rooms. Its length of 10m is also very typical, and probably reflects the use of the 5m perch unit of measurement in laying out building plots in medieval towns. As in the Guildhall, the partition wall between the central hall and the parlour has been removed, together